J

428.1 McMillan, Bruce
MC
          Dry or wet?

$11.88

Dry or

For my Springvale librarians

Library of Congress Cataloging in Publication Data   McMillan, Bruce.   Dry or wet? Summary: Paired photographs illustrate the concept of wet and dry.
1. English language—Synonyms and antonyms—Juvenile literature. [1. English language—Synonyms and antonyms—Pictorial works]   I. Title.
PE1591.M434   1987   428.1   86-27345   ISBN 0-688-07100-7   ISBN 0-688-07101-5 (lib. bdg.)

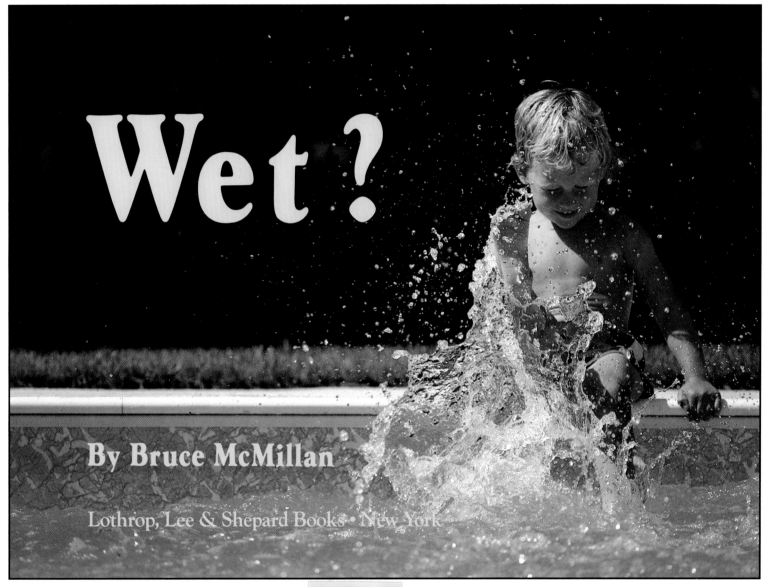

Wet?

By Bruce McMillan

Lothrop, Lee & Shepard Books • New York

6

7

8

9

10

13

15

16

17

18

19

20

21

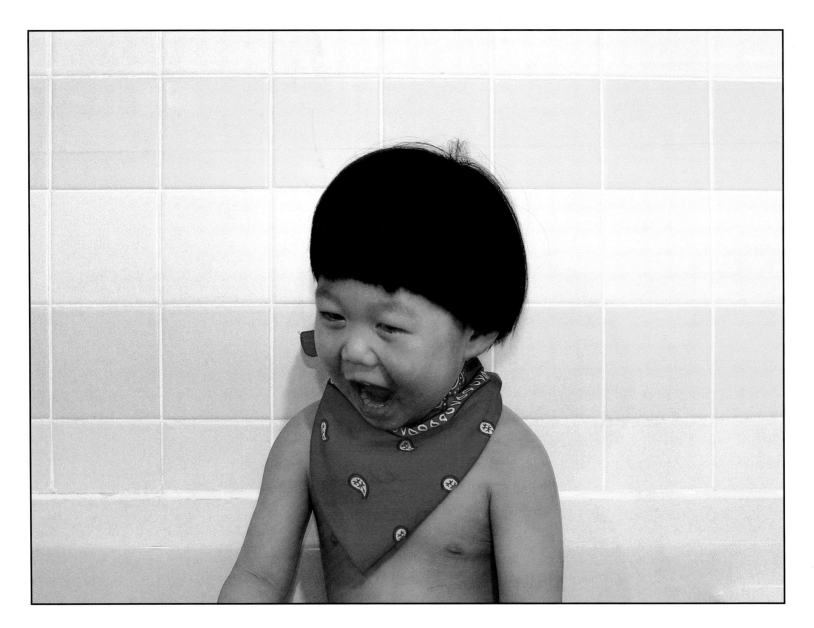

22

23

24

25

26

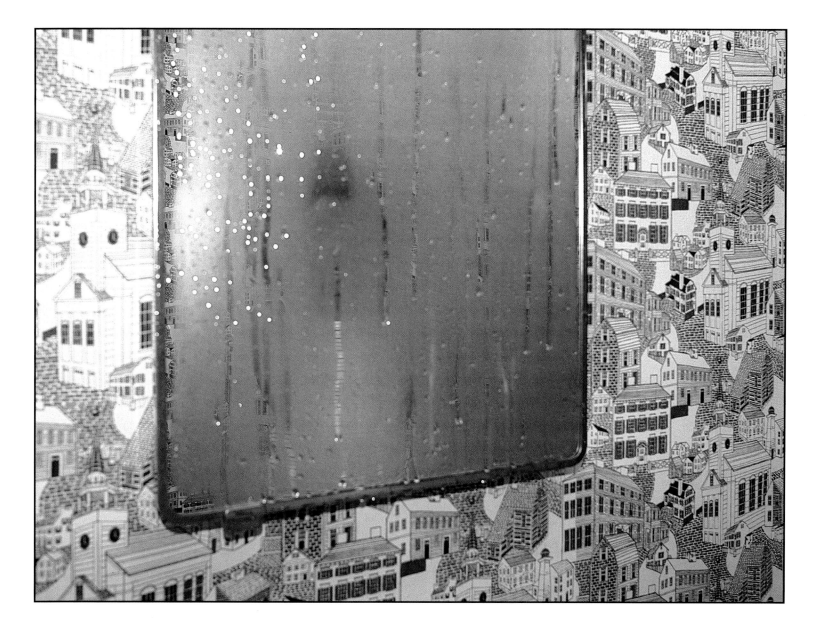

27

28

About This Book

There are many ways *Dry or Wet?* can be used to increase a child's ability to use words effectively. Identifying what is dry and what is wet in the pictures is only the beginning. Some of the other "wet" words that fit the context of the photographs are SPLASH, DOWNPOUR, SPRAY, SHOWER, SPURT, STREAM, GUSH, MOIST, DAMP, STEAM, FOGGY. Other "dry" words are WATERLESS, SUNNY, TOWEL-DRY, SOAK UP, WIPE, THIRSTY, WITHERED, WILTED, PARCHED. And, of course, many colorful expressions could be used to describe what is happening: for instance, the girl on page 16 could be described as HIGH AND DRY until she's SOAKED TO THE SKIN by the sprinkler on page 17. The possibilities are endless. The suggestions above are meant to get you started!

Two children's librarians from the Springvale, Maine, Public Library, Joanne Vermette and Susan Bshara, suggested that I work with words that express things that children can feel. The concepts of wet and dry were among their suggestions. This book came to life when I met the wonderful children who appear in the photographs. Thanks to Joanne and Sue for the idea, and thanks to the boys and girls who seemed to enjoy every minute of our playful shooting sessions. They are, in order of appearance, H. Parker Sowles, Emily Blanchard, Marisa Sowles, Justin King, Jayne McCullough, Niccolo Bruno-Hymoff, and Anna Matthews Hayden. Thanks also go to Phoebe, the Dalmatian, who was a good sport about it all.

A special vote of thanks is due the several people who helped behind the scenes: Children's librarian Shari Turner, and parents H. William and Jeannette Sowles, Susan and David Blanchard, John and Sylvia Sowles, Judith Hansen, Mary and Jack McCullough, Holly Bruno and Ira Hymoff, Kim Matthews, and Phoebe's owner-parents, Louise and Red Sullivan.

The photographs were taken using Nikon F2 and FE2 motor-driven cameras, with 28, 50, 105, and 200mm Nikkor lenses. The film used was Kodachrome 64, processed by Eastman Kodak.